PERSONAL BEST

TRACK AND FIELD

CLIVE GIFFORD

PowerKiDS press™

New York

Published in 2009 by The Rosen Publishing Group Inc.
29 East 21st Street, New York, NY 10010

First Edition

Managing Editor: Rasha Elsaeed
Produced by Tall Tree Ltd
Editor: Jon Richards
Designer: Ben Ruocco
Photographer: Michael Wicks
Consultant: Jamie Bath

Library of Congress Cataloging-in-Publication Data

Gifford, Clive.
  Track and field / Clive Gifford. — 1st ed.
     p. cm. — (Personal best)
  Includes index.
  ISBN 978-1-4042-4442-9 (library binding)
 1. Track and field—Juvenile literature. I. Title.
  GV1060.55.G54 2008
  796.42—dc22
                          2007042984

Picture credits
All photographs taken by Michael Wicks, except;
5 Paul Hanna/Reuters/Corbis, 12 tr Dreamstime.com/William Farquhar,
29 cl Dreamstime.com/Jim Parkin

Disclaimer
In the preparation of this book, care has been exercised with regard to advice,
activities and techniques. However, when the reader is learning or engaged in
a sport or utilizing a piece of equipment, the reader should get advice from an
expert and follow the manufacturer's instructions. The publisher cannot be, and
is not liable for, any loss or injury the reader may sustain.

Manufactured in China

CONTENTS

WHAT IS TRACK AND FIELD?

Track and field is an exciting and demanding collection of disciplines involving running, jumping, and throwing. Many of its events date from the ancient world. The ancient Greek Olympics, which began over 2,700 years ago, included sprint races, a long jump, and forms of discus and javelin. Today, track and field athletics is one of the most popular parts of the Olympic games, and its champions, such as Carl Lewis, Carolina Kluft, and Sebastian Coe, are international stars.

TRACK AND FIELD

Track and field—also known simply as "athletics"—is so called because of the way the sport is split into two types or classes of event. Track events are mostly individual running races held over different distances around a track. Some events involve clearing hurdles or barriers, and others, called relays, involve teams of four runners. Field events are throwing competitions, such as the discus, and jumping disciplines, such as the high jump.

Whatever event you take part in, you will need skill, commitment, hard work, and plenty of training to succeed. Challenging yourself with track and field events at school, local sports clubs, and competitions is also exciting, fun, and rewarding. Athletes at all levels strive to improve so that they can achieve their fastest-ever times, longest throws, or longest and highest jumps. This is known as a personal best, or "PB."

Clothing

Clothing for an athlete is relatively simple. This athlete is wearing a lightweight vest over a cotton T-shirt for extra warmth while training. She is wearing lightweight shorts and short cotton socks, which absorb sweat. Other essential items include a tracksuit to keep you warm, a small towel to dry your hands and face, and a water bottle, all kept in a sports bag.

Footwear varies for the different track and field events. These sprint shoes are known as spikes due to the short spikes fitted to the sole underneath the ball of the foot. These spikes help to provide grip.

Shoes for the shot put, discus, and hammer throwing events tend not to have spikes. Instead, they have smooth rubber soles, which allow the thrower to turn easily.

STADIUM AND OFFICIALS

A track and field stadium is dominated by an oval track, which usually measures 400 meters and has a minimum of eight marked-out lanes. The track surface is usually a form of plastic or rubber and provides good grip for runners. The field events are held in their own areas, which are usually inside the track. Officials make sure that events run smoothly. Their roles include judging on false starts and close finishes in races, as well as measuring the distances of jumps or throws.

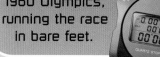

hammer

high jump

long jump and triple jump

pole vault

shot put

javelin

The U.S. athlete, Lauryn Williams, (far left), dips across the line to win the women's 100-meter race at the World Championships in Helsinki. Her winning time was 10.93 seconds.

SPRINT START

The sprints are races held over short distances, where the athletes try to run as quickly as they can. The most common sprint races are the 100 meters and 200 meters. In indoor and outdoor track and field for juniors under 11, the 100 meters is usually replaced with the 60-meter sprint. Whatever the distance, every sprinter needs as good a start as possible.

Starting blocks support the sprinters' feet at the start and give their feet something to push against. This helps to increase the sprinters' power as they drive away at the start.

This sprinter prepares for her race start by placing her hands a little wider than shoulder-width apart. Her fingertips press down onto the track in a bridged position just behind the start line. Her arms are straight but the elbows are not locked.

GETTING A GOOD START

A good start cannot win you a sprint race by itself, but a race can certainly be lost by a poor, slow start. A sprinter needs to be balanced in the starting blocks and totally focused on the starter's signals. The first, a call of "On your marks," sees the sprinter enter the starting blocks. The second call of "Set" sees the sprinter get into the starting position. A sprinter then needs excellent reactions and technique to respond to the starter's third signal—a pistol shot or shout of "Go!"—as quickly as possible.

1 When she hears the call of "On your marks," the sprinter goes to her starting blocks, kneels down, and gets her feet into position on the footpads.

2 She next gets her hands into position just behind the start line. Her shoulders are held a little distance behind her hands.

3 The sprinter adopts the starting position at the "Set" command. Her hips rise, tilting her body so that her shoulders are above her hands.

4 As the starter signals "Go!," the sprinter drives hard off her starting blocks, but keeps low. Her rear leg comes through to take her first race stride, while her right arm is thrown back and her left arm pumps forward.

5 The sprinter takes her second race stride. She keeps her body position low with her head looking at the track some distance ahead. Her arms pump back and forth, passing close by her body.

FALSE STARTS AND REACTION TIMES

A good start is essential, but if a sprinter moves out of the blocks and starts before the starter's signal, they make a false start and the race has to be restarted. In local competitions, officials judge false starts by eye. At major championships, electronic systems determine how fast a sprinter's feet leave the footpads of the starting blocks after the starter's gun—this is known as reaction time. A sprinter with a reaction time of less than 0.12 seconds is considered to have made a false start. After one false start occurs, the next false start by any sprinter will mean that runner is disqualified from taking part in the race.

Staggered start

These 200-meter runners (below) are on their marks. Their starting blocks are staggered so that each runner has the same distance to cover when running around the bend of the track. When the starter orders "Set," the runners raise themselves into their starting position. Their focus is on their track lane, not on a rival runner in a lane ahead. Reacting to the start of the race, the sprinters drive out from their blocks. Their hands leave the track first, the body position is low, and the back legs come through to take the first stride.

SPRINTING

After the start, a sprinter accelerates and gradually raises his or her body into an upright position. A sprinter will reach top speed during the middle of a short sprint race. From then onward, the sprinter will try to maintain his or her speed and good running posture and style right up to the finishing line.

SPRINTING TECHNIQUE

A sprinter's first stride in a race is the shortest, and the stride length increases as the sprinter accelerates into the race. The rate at which he or she makes strides is known as cadence, and this also increases as the sprinter reaches top speed.

A sprinter's legs drive with a high knee action that sees the thigh rise parallel to the ground. The front leg is stretched forward by the time it touches the track. The leading foot paws at the ground as it lands, helping to pull the rest of the athlete forward. A sprinter tries to run tall, with a high hip position underneath his or her body, which, along with the head, points straight down the track. The arms should pump smoothly back and forth, and not across the body.

This sprinter runs tall and relaxed, with her head upright and her eyes focused down her lane. Her hands are relaxed with fingers loosely curled. Her right leg drives forward with a high knee action, and as that leg comes forward, her left leg is extended behind her, pushing off the track on its toes.

Knee lift

A vital part of sprinting is the high knee lift. This sprinter is performing an exaggerated knee lift drill. Keeping her back upright, she stands on the ball of her other foot and drives her knee up high, past the point where her thigh is parallel to the track. She is also pumping her arms at the same time.

This runner sprints around the bend. She leans fractionally into the bend and concentrates on running smoothly, with her head up and looking forward.

RUNNING THE BEND

Sprinters must stay in their lanes throughout the race, otherwise they will be disqualified. This can prove a problem for beginners looking to power around a bend in the 200 meters or 400 meters, where their speed tends to force them to the outside of their lanes. Sprinters often counteract this by leaning into the bend and sometimes, pressing their inside shoulders slightly forward. These techniques help to keep them on the inside of their lanes, which is the shortest route around the track.

A sprinter is judged to have run out of his or her lane not only if a foot lands inside another lane, but also if a foot touches either of the lines marking the lane. Running out of a lane leads to disqualification.

FAST FINISH

The last section of a sprint race sees athletes trying to maintain their sprinting technique. They try to keep their shoulders down and their upper bodies as still as possible. They avoid rolling from side to side and strive to run through the finishing line. Many races are lost by sprinters tensing up or easing their pace as they approach the finish line.

This sprinter shows good timing to thrust his arms back and his chest forward to cross the finishing line. To finish a race, the line only has to be crossed by the sprinter's body, not their arms and legs.

RELAY RUNNING

Relays are team events featuring four runners, all of whom run the same distance, known as a leg. They run with a baton that must be passed from runner to runner. The 4x100-meter sprint is the most common relay for younger athletes. Teenagers and adults may also run the longer 4x400 meters.

At the start, runners must make sure that the baton is not touching the ground across the line.

THE 4X100-METER RELAY

A 4x100-meter relay race requires expert timing and understanding between teammates, and this only comes from lots of hard practice. The baton is gripped firmly by the first runner, who sprints around the first bend and passes the baton on to the second runner.

The exchange must take place within the changeover zone. This is a 20-meter-long box that is marked out on the running track. The second runner must have the baton under control when he or she leaves the zone. Failure to do so means that the team is disqualified.

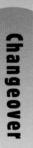

Changeover

1 The receiver has watched her teammate coming toward her and has timed her start so that she is inside the changeover zone as her teammate arrives.

2 The incoming runner has responsibility for the baton changeover since she can see what is going on. She will let the receiver know that the baton is arriving.

3 The incoming runner places the baton into her teammate's hand. She tries not to slow down until the baton is under the receiver's control.

4 The receiver is now in full control of the baton and drives away as fast as she can in order to complete her leg of the relay race.

Changeover zones

This diagram shows the four changeover zones marked out on a typical track. Before each changeover zone there is a 10-meter-long acceleration zone. The receiving runner is allowed to stand in this zone and start running before receiving the baton in the changeover zone.

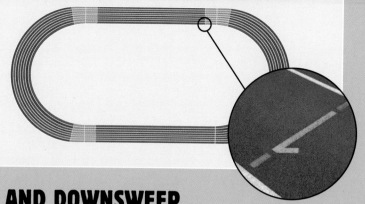

1 In the downsweep, the receiver stretches a hand back with the palm upward.

2 The incoming runner sweeps the baton down into the receiver's hand and only lets go when the baton is firmly grasped.

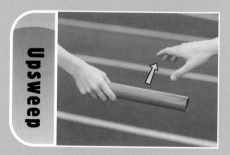

1 The upsweep method sees the incoming runner sweep the baton up into the receiver's hand.

UPSWEEP AND DOWNSWEEP

For maximum speed in the 4x100 meters, the baton is passed blind, with the receiver facing ahead. There are two methods of passing the baton when the receiver is looking ahead and not at the baton. They are called the downsweep and the upsweep.

THE 4X400-METER RELAY

A 4x400-meter race features a start similar to a regular 400 meters. The first runner completes his or her leg and hands over the baton to the second runner. The second runner must complete the first 100 meters of the leg in his or her lane and can then "break" and head toward the inside lane of the track. The second and third changeovers occur with the runners waiting to run lined-up along the finishing line waiting for their teammates to arrive with the baton.

2 The baton is placed in the "V" formed by the thumb and palm of the receiver's hand.

HURDLING

Hurdling involves jumping over barriers, called hurdles, during a sprint. It requires great skill to clear the hurdles quickly and successfully.

HURDLING EVENTS

Hurdling events are usually held over distances varying from 60 meters indoors to the 400-meter hurdles. The most common hurdling events are the men's 110-meter hurdles and the 100-meter hurdles for women. Both of these feature ten hurdles spaced evenly along the track.

THE HURDLES

Most hurdles are adjustable, and their height is set to suit the age and ability of the athletes taking part. In your earliest hurdling training, your coach may set the hurdles to their lowest possible height. Hurdles are designed to topple over easily if hit by an athlete, providing they are jumped from the correct side. Never attempt to jump a hurdle from the wrong side, because you can cause yourself a serious injury.

DID YOU KNOW?

The U.S. athlete, Ed Moses, won the 400-meter hurdles at the 1976 and 1984 Olympics (the U.S. boycotted the 1980 games). He was unbeaten for 122 races in a row over almost 10 years!

Viewed from the front, you can see how the hurdlers run in the middle of their lanes as they approach hurdles. Their front legs are already rising high before their rear legs leave the track. The front legs are thrown over the hurdles with the trailing legs brought around and over the hurdles. Hurdlers have to be careful to prevent their legs from trailing around the outside of the hurdles. If this is spotted by officials, the hurdler will be disqualified.

1 Two athletes sprint hard as they approach the next hurdles on the track. They make sure their stride pattern is correct as they take their second-from-last stride before the hurdle.

2 Into their last stride, the hurdlers land on the legs that will drive them up and over the hurdles. This is the rear or trailing leg. The hurdlers look to stay balanced and with their shoulders pointing straight ahead.

3 As the hurdle approaches, the leading legs bend high and lift as the trailing legs drive up and forward off the ground. The arms on the same side as the trailing legs drive forward also, to keep the hurdlers balanced.

4 As the front legs clear the hurdles, the trailing legs are pulled up and bent at the knees with the feet turned outward. They are then brought forward and around to the front.

5 The trailing legs clear the hurdles just before landing. The hurdlers aim to get their leading legs down onto the track as quickly as possible to help maintain their pace.

6 After landing, the arms on the trailing sides are swung back. These help the trailing legs swing forward quickly. Staying upright and looking down their lane, the hurdlers sprint away.

HURDLE TRAINING

Hurdlers have to work extremely hard in training to develop a smooth hurdling style. A key part of their technique is building a good rhythm of strides between each hurdle. These strides must maintain a hurdler's pace while getting the athlete in the perfect position to take off to clear the next hurdle. Watch experienced hurdlers in action—their running action is hardly interrupted by clearing each hurdle.

A hurdler practicing her technique over hurdles placed close together.

15

DISTANCE RUNNING

There are many races run over longer distances than the sprints. These are usually divided up into long-distance events and middle-distance races. Middle-distance races are run over 800 meters and 1,500 meters.

These two middle-distance runners (below) run along one of the straights of the track. They run on the balls of their feet and lift their front legs with a high knee action. The lower parts of their front legs stretch out and make contact with the ground. As they do so, the rear legs begin swinging through to take the next step.

MIDDLE-DISTANCE RUNNING

Competitive 800-meter races see the runners start from a staggered position on the bend across the track. After the first 100 meters, however, they are allowed to break out of their lanes and head toward the inside lane. The 1,500 meters sees athletes line up along a curved start line, and after the race has started, they "break" into the inside lane.

Middle-distance runners concentrate on developing a relaxed running style that they can repeat even when they are tired. Runners usually aim for an even pace that leaves them with enough energy to finish the race with a sprint.

Head and shoulders steady and relaxed.

Arms swing back and forward close by body with elbows bent at right angles.

Body is upright and pointing toward the running direction.

Hands are relaxed and not bunched into a fist.

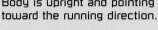
Running start

1 When they hear "On your marks," the runners stand with their weight over their front feet, which are just behind the start line. Their knees are bent and they are leaning forward.

2 When they hear the starter's pistol or "Go!," the athletes forcefully drive away off their front legs. Their back legs swing forward to take the first stride.

LONG-DISTANCE RUNNING

Longer events, usually those of 5,000 meters or more, are known as long-distance races. These include cross-country competitions, which see athletes run around a prepared course including hills and dips. On the track, the most common long-distance races are the 5,000 meters and the 10,000 meters.

The ultimate running challenge is the marathon. Measuring 42.2 kilometers—that's over 26 miles!— it is an incredible test of endurance with elite runners completing this huge distance in just over two hours. The marathon is held on a prepared course, usually on roads. At the Olympics, runners complete it by running into a stadium and performing one lap of the track.

THE STEEPLECHASE

The steeplechase is a track race run at major competitions over a distance of 3,000 meters, although 1,500-meter and 2,000-meter steeplechase events are often held. In the full 3,000-meter event, a runner has to jump and clear barriers 28 times and a water jump seven times. These barriers are solid and cannot be knocked over by athletes, but their top surface can be stepped on if the athlete cannot hurdle them.

As a pack of middle-distance runners rounds the bend, the athlete in red and yellow finds himself "boxed in" by the other runners. He is unable to move out and attack the front.

Rounding the final bend of a middle-distance race, one runner starts to make his move. He pulls out from the inside lane to reach the shoulder of the lead runner, and looks to race past him to take the lead.

Steeplechase

2 As her front leg clears the barrier, she brings her rear leg around and forward. Her arms are out to help her balance, and she aims to get her front foot back on the track as quickly as possible to continue running.

1 The athlete approaches one of the barriers in a steeplechase race. She drives off her rear leg, while her front leg is lifted high at the knee to travel over the barrier first.

LONG JUMP

The long jump is a test of speed, timing, and explosive power. A long jumper sprints up a narrow track area called a runway with as much pace under control as possible. The jumper's aim is to turn forward speed into a long and powerful jump.

THE RUN UP

The long jump run up can be split into three stages— acceleration, running upright, and gather strides. The first sees the jumper sprint hard from a standing start. The jumper then aims to reach top speed with the body and hands relaxed and the head upright. The third stage sees the athlete make his or her last few strides.

THE JUMPING AREA

The long jump features a runway made of the same substance as a running track, which is at least 43.7 yards (40 meters) long and about feet 3.3 yards (3 m) wide. Just in front of the sandpit, which in major competitions is usually feet 9.8 yards (9 m) long, is the take-off board. It is white, placed across the runway, and approximately inches 8 in. (20 cm) wide. Athletes are allowed to step onto but not past the board with the foot they use to jump off. A layer of modeling clay is usually placed along the take-off board's front edge. This shows any imprints made by a foot overstepping, which results in a foul jump.

The jump above is a good one with the ball of the athlete's foot on the white take-off board but not touching the green modeling clay. The second jump (below), with the foot well over the board, will be signaled a foul jump.

MAXIMIZING DISTANCE

Jumps are measured from the front edge of the take-off board to the nearest mark made in the sand by the jumper. This means a jumper wants to make his or her first mark in the sand as far ahead as possible. It also means that a jumper wants to take-off from as near to the sandpit as possible, without creating a foul jump. Raw speed down the runway is no use unless it is under control and the athlete is accurate with the run-up. A jumper works out the length of the run-up with a coach and then measures it out extremely carefully.

1 This long jumper approaches the take-off board. He has measured his run-up accurately, so that his last stride is slightly shorter than usual.

2 The athlete's take-off foot contacts the board with the whole foot. At the moment of contact, the jumper's shoulders are slightly behind his hips.

3 The jumper drives up explosively. To perform the hang kick well, he will extend his arms and legs outward so that he appears to hang in the air.

4 As he lands, the jumper lets his legs buckle, bending his knees. This will help drive him forward so that he does not disturb the sand behind his feet.

Hang, hitch, or stride

Once a long jumper has taken off, he or she wants as much time in the air as possible. There are a number of different techniques a long jumper can use once in the air. Two of the most common are the hitch kick and the hang kick. The hitch kick sees the jumper make an exaggerated cycling movement with his or her legs, and with the arms held overhead. The hang style (see left) involves the jumper extending the arms and legs before swinging them forward.

This jumper's efforts have been ruined by his landing. Because he was unable to throw himself forward when he landed, he has leaned back, sat in the sand, and put his right arm back to steady himself. His jump will be measured from his right handprint, losing him a lot of distance.

HIGH JUMP

The high jump is a contest of grace, flexibility, and explosive power. A jumper must make a rhythmical run-up and approach before exploding off the take-off foot to clear the high-jump bar. The best adult jumpers can clear heights taller than themselves.

Scissors jump

1 Coming from an angle of 45 degrees, the jumper makes his run up to the bar on the balls of his feet with a springy step. He plants his outside foot and bends it at the knee. The other leg, the leading leg, starts to swing up.

2 As the jumper springs off his outside leg to make the jump, his leading leg is driven up high to clear the bar. His arms drive upward and to around shoulder height. These help to create more lift.

3 Keeping his back as straight as possible, the jumper brings his outside leg up and over the bar. The leading leg is forced downward onto the crash mat. A good scissors jump should see the athlete land on both feet.

THE HIGH JUMP BAR

The high jump is a bar rested on supports that are fitted to two uprights approximately yards 4.4 yards (4 meters) apart. Behind the supports is a giant crash mat, which jumpers fall onto safely. A high jumper has to clear the bar without knocking it off.

There are many techniques used to clear the bar. The simplest is the scissors kick, where two legs are lifted up and down in a scissorslike motion. In the 1960s, Dick Fosbury revolutionized high jumping with his Fosbury flop technique (see right). This is now used by most jumpers, but only if there is a crash mat.

Here, you can see the upside-down, J-shaped path that the high-jumper takes when performing the Fosbury flop. Work with your coach to devise your ideal run-up.

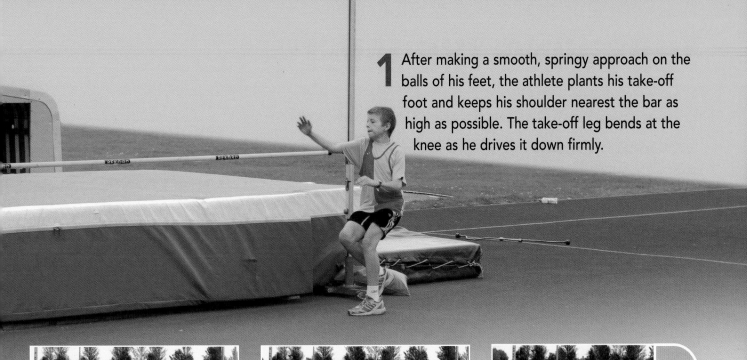

1 After making a smooth, springy approach on the balls of his feet, the athlete plants his take-off foot and keeps his shoulder nearest the bar as high as possible. The take-off leg bends at the knee as he drives it down firmly.

Fosbury flop

2 The athlete makes an explosive leap almost straight upward. The knee of his leading leg drives high and the arms pump upward too, to help generate extra lift.

3 Keeping his back straight, the jumper's shoulders travel past the bar. He raises his hips and pulls his heels in. Top-flight high jumpers look over their shoulders as they travel over the bar.

4 The jumper's hips rise and once past the bar, he flexes his hips and raises his legs so they rise up and over the high-jump bar. Clearing the bar smoothly, he lands on the crash mat.

COMPETITION JUMPING

In competition, high jumpers are given 90 seconds to complete each attempt. They are usually given three attempts at each height. If they fail to clear the bar in three attempts, then they are out of the competition. As jumpers succeed at a height, the bar is raised. This is usually done in units of 1.2 or 2 inches (3 or 5 centimeters), although in attempting to set a record, some competitions see the bar raised only by 0.4 in. (1 cm). The winner of a high-jump competition is the jumper who has cleared the greatest height. If two or more athletes have cleared the same height but no higher, then the winner is the jumper with the fewest failures beforehand.

Viewed from behind, you can see how in the last stages of the jump, the jumper brings his head forward to help raise his feet over the bar.

THROWING THE JAVELIN

Developed from spear-throwing competitions thousands of years ago, the javelin is one of the most popular field events. Although a javelin is light in weight—an adult male javelin is 1.8 pounds (800 grams) and an adult female javelin is 1.3 lb. (600 g)—great skill, power, and timing are needed to throw it long distances.

ON THE RUNWAY

Unlike the shot put, discus, and hammer, which take place in a circle, javelin throws are made on a runway that is 4.4 yards (4 meters) wide and more than 33 yards (30 meters) long. At the end of the runway is a curved line known as the scratch line. This marks out the end of the runway and the start of the javelin landing area. If the athlete steps over the scratch line, then the throw will be invalid.

This athlete has misjudged his run-up and overstepped the scratch line at the front of the runway. His throw is invalid and will not count.

The grip

Gripping the javelin is important because it is the grip that transfers the power from the throw into the javelin's flight. Here are the three main ways you can grip the javelin. Work with your coach to see which grip suits you best.

The middle finger grip sees the javelin lie on the palm of the hand, where it is gripped by the thumb and middle finger.

The forefinger and middle finger are placed on the sides of the javelin on the edge of the back of the cord grip. This is called the V, or claw, grip.

The forefinger, or Finnish, grip sees the forefinger of the hand placed behind the cord binding on the javelin.

THROWING ACTION

The javelin is a long shaft made of metal, wood, or artificial materials with a pointed metal end. It must be gripped on the part of its length that is wrapped in cord. It must also be thrown up and over the shoulder.

In simple terms, the javelin action starts with the athlete at the far end of the runway. The javelin is lifted overhead during the carry phase as the athlete builds up speed along the runway. Then, the javelin is pulled back during the withdrawal phase, and the legs crossover and move into the delivery stride. The javelin is pulled past the body and released. When it is timed well, much of the power in a good javelin throw comes from the athlete's back and legs, and also the arm.

The angle of release is crucial since a javelin's front tip, called the point, must touch the ground first when it lands. The top two throws, where another part of the javelin other than the point landed first, are invalid. The bottom throw is a legal one.

The throw

1 The athlete has already moved off from his standing start. He carries the javelin with a high arm and the javelin parallel with the ground, pointing to the target.

2 He begins to withdraw the javelin by taking his arm backward. His chest and shoulders begin to turn from their forward-facing position to the side.

3 With his arm extended backward, the javelin is fully withdrawn. His chest is pointing to the side and his shoulders are in line with the target.

4 The athlete performs the crossover stride with the leg on his throwing arm side stepping across his body. This stride will enable him to lean back a little

5 With his front leg braced, the athlete's back arches and he starts to turn his hips forward. The elbow is kept high as he starts to pull the javelin through.

6 With his chest forward-facing, the thrower's arm is pulled through. The javelin is released at an approximate angle to the ground of 45 degrees.

SHOT PUTTING

The shot is a heavy metal ball thrown from inside a circle using a one-handed body and arm action known as putting. Lighter shot are used for children and in training, and they are sometimes made from artificial materials.

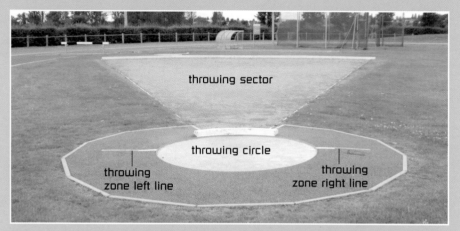

throwing sector

throwing circle

throwing zone left line

throwing zone right line

The throwing circle is a 2.335-yard-wide (2.135-meter-wide) circle from which the shot is thrown. To be a valid throw, the shot must land inside the 40-degree-wide throwing sector marked out on either side by lines.

PUTTING PROCEDURE

Shot putters enter the back of the throwing circle with the shot cradled safely in both hands. When they are ready, they get into the starting position in the throwing circle and then make their throw. They must not leave the throwing circle until the shot has landed, and then it must be from the back of the circle. Overbalancing and stepping over the front of the throwing circle will result in a foul throw.

The grip

The shot is cradled in the hand with the three middle fingers so that it is above and not touching the palm. The little finger and thumb touch the shot's sides to help steady it in position.

This image (below) shows the shot putter taking a crouched stance at the start of a standing throw. He will turn and drive upward from his rear leg to release the shot with a fully extended arm.

The shot is nestled into the neck and tucked under the side of the chin (right).

The shot putter uses the wooden stopboard (also called a toeboard) at the front of the throwing circle to brace the front foot against as they complete the throw (left). This can help to stop the thrower from overbalancing.

O'BRIEN AND ROTATIONAL TECHNIQUES

Beginners to the shot often start with the standing throw. Their feet are fixed in one position and they throw the shot by rising from a low to high body and arm position. The next stage is the linear, or O'Brien, technique named after its devisor, Parry O'Brien, who was the first man to throw over 20.7 yards (19 meters). This sees the athlete start at the back of the circle and then move across it to generate maximum thrust to send the shot away. The rotational technique is more complex and relies on excellent footwork and timing. It sees you spin inside the circle, pivoting around one foot to build up speed, before exploding up and into the throw.

1 This athlete is about to put the shot using the O'Brien technique, moving in a straight line across the throwing circle. She extends her arm upward gripping the shot before bringing it into her neck.

2 The thrower leans facing the back of the circle with the shot cradled in her neck and her nonthrowing arm out for balance. Her back faces the direction in which she is going to throw.

3 The athlete lifts her front leg as she drives off her back leg and makes a low hop across the circle. As she moves across the circle, she aims to plant her front foot next to the stopboard.

4 With her front leg braced, the athlete drives up and her body turns to face the front. Her arm extends quickly and drives the shot away, releasing it with a flick of the fingers.

Having completed her throw, this athlete steps out of the back of the throwing circle. The front and back halves of the circle are marked by the two straight white lines.

25

DISCUS THROWING

The discus is an aerodynamic flying disc that throwers propel with a vigorous arm and body action. Timing and good technique are more important than brute strength to send the discus flying away well.

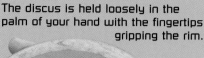

The discus is held loosely in the palm of your hand with the fingertips gripping the rim.

PRELIMINARY SWINGS

The basic technique for beginners is the standing throw. This requires several preliminary swings of the discus back and forth to build up rhythm and momentum. The thrower stands with the outside of his or her front foot facing the front of the circle, feet apart, and with the knees slightly flexed. With the discus in the correct grip, the throwing arm swings back as the thrower turns at the waist and then swings forward. The swing goes from a low position at the backswing to a high position at the front of the swing.

As your throwing hand swings forward on your preliminary swings, get your nonthrowing hand underneath the discus to support it.

1 After performing the preliminary swings, this thrower begins his final swing. He swings his hips to take the discus a little farther back than before.

2 Turning on the ball of his back foot, the thrower's body turns rapidly toward the front. The discus is released when his shoulders are facing forward.

Standing throw

3 The discus flies away from the thrower's hand with his forefinger touching it last. He follows through with the arm and does not step out of the circle.

Discus rules

Discus throwing takes place in a throwing circle slightly larger than the shot putting circle, but with similar rules applying. Throwers enter and exit the circle from the back. They must not touch the area outside the front of the circle after throwing, otherwise a foul throw will be awarded.

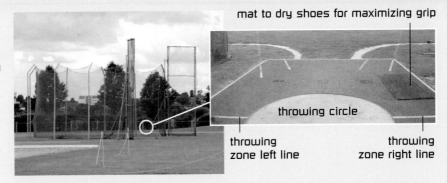

mat to dry shoes for maximizing grip

throwing circle

throwing zone left line

throwing zone right line

Discus throws take place in a cage made of nets to catch wayward throws. In the middle is a 2.7-yard-wide (2.5-meter-wide) throwing circle with no stopboard but with a 40-degree throwing sector marked in front of the circle.

THROWING TIPS

The discus event mixes strength with timing and flexibility. Throwers develop a rhythm with the preliminary swings so that as much momentum as possible is built up before the discus is released. A vital part of transferring as much momentum into the throw is to brace your nonthrowing side as your throwing arm comes through. Being braced with your foot planted firmly gives the rest of your body a platform to move against, helping to create extra power. Finally, work hard with your coach at practice to make sure that you are releasing the disc at the right angle. A discus released at too sharp or shallow an angle will fly a much shorter distance.

These images show the moments before and after the discus release. The thrower presses his fingers down on the edge of the disc as it is released. This helps it to spin away and fly smoothly through the air.

The next step up from the standing throw is the rotational discus throw. The athlete begins at the back of the circle and then makes one-and-a-half turns as he moves across the circle. He winds his throwing arm so that he releases the discus with a great deal of speed and force, but with excellent timing to propel it across long distances.

OTHER EVENTS

There are a number of other events that you can take part in as you get older and gain experience. These include the triple jump and hammer throw, the spectacular pole vault, and the decathlon.

HAMMER THROWING

The hammer is a heavy ball on a metal chain that is thrown inside a circle protected by a safety cage. The men's hammer weighs 16 lb. (7.26 kg) and the women's weighs 8.8 lb. (4 kg). The athlete winds up a big throw by swinging the hammer around and around, building up speed before releasing the hammer.

The hammer grip sees the left hand hold the hammer handle with the right hand closing over it.

Hammer

1 The thrower starts at the back of the circle. The hammer is placed on the ground to the right of his right foot.

2 The hammer is swung in front of the thrower's body as he rotates on the ball of his right foot and the heel of his left foot.

The hammer swings around on the chain a little behind the thrower. The thrower makes several turns to build up momentum.

3

4 On the final turn, the thrower drives his legs up, following with his arms, and releases the hammer at its highest point.

5 The hammer is released over the thrower's left shoulder so that it flies up and forward. Ideally, it is released at 45 degrees.

6 The thrower takes care not to lose balance and step out of the front of the circle. This would cause a foul throw.

TRIPLE JUMP

Usually performed in the same area and pit as the long jump, the triple jump sees the athlete power down the runway before performing a hop, then a step, and finally a jump. The athlete aims to make the three movements as smooth and fluid as possible in what is a technically demanding event.

HEPTATHLON AND DECATHLON

The ultimate challenge for versatile athletes is to take part in the seven-event heptathlon for women or the ten-event decathlon for men. These are held over two days. Day one sees decathletes perform the 100 meters, long jump, shot put, high jump, and 400 meters, and heptathletes perform the 100-meter hurdles, high jump, shot put, and 200 meters. Day two for decathletes involves the 110-meter hurdles, discus, pole vault, javelin, and finally, the 1,500 meters. On day two, heptathletes perform the long jump, javelin, and the 800 meters.

Pole vault

During the pole vault, an athlete uses a flexible pole to propel him or her over a bar. It starts with the vaulter running down a runway holding the pole. The vaulter plants the pole into a hole called the vaulting box. The pole bends and then straightens, carrying the vaulter up with it. The vaulter swings his or her hips overhead to travel feet-first over the bar.

A pole vaulter holds his pole high on the runway before attempting a vault over the bar. He will build up good speed on the runway before planting the pole and vaulting over.

Triple jump

1 After making his approach run, this triple jumper makes his hop with his trailing leg swung back.

2 The runner aims to land on the foot he hopped off of, with his whole foot making contact with the track.

3 Making the step, the take-off leg trails behind the jumper. His other leg is bent at the knee and held high so that his thigh is parallel to the runway.

4 Completing the step and entering the jump phase, the athlete swings both of his arms forward as he drives off his take-off leg. His other leg is kept high.

5 The take-off leg is brought quickly through so that both feet are well ahead of the athlete. The landing is similar to the long jump (see pages 18–19).

Glossary

back straight The straight part of the track that is farthest away from the finishing line.

baton The short tube passed in a relay race between runners in the same team.

boxed-in When a middle- or long-distance runner is trapped from moving out and ahead during a race by other runners around him or her.

cage The safety net surrounding the hammer and discus throwing circles.

changeover zone Also known as the take-over zone, this is a marked out area of the track inside of which the baton in a relay race must be exchanged between team members.

decathlon The ten discipline event for male athletes that is held over two days.

disqualification To be removed from an event or to lose your finishing position in an event if you have broken the rules while you are taking part.

Fosbury flop A popular type of high-jump technique, which sees an athlete jump over the bar head first and with their back facing down.

foul jump An illegal long or triple jump due to the athlete overstepping the take-off board or breaking some other rule.

foul throw An illegal hammer, discus, shot put, or javelin throw due to the throw landing outside of the throwing area or due to another rule being broken.

hang A flight technique used in the long jump.

heat An early race or running of a field event in which the fastest race-finishers or the best throwers or jumpers advance to the next round or the final of the competition.

heptathlon The seven discipline event for women that is held over two days.

hitch A flight technique used in the long jump.

O'Brien technique A type of shot putting style where the shot putter starts at the back of the circle and drives across it.

pack The main group of runners in a middle- and long-distance race.

personal best An athlete's best-ever time, height, or distance for an event.

scratch line The line on the javelin, long jump, and triple jump runways that must not be crossed by an athlete's foot during or after the attempt.

staggered start Starting blocks placed in such a way that when runners run a race that includes a bend, they each cover the same distance.

stamina The ability to keep performing hard for an extended period of time

starting blocks A pair of angled supports for the feet that help to increase the power of a sprinter from a crouch start.

stopboard The wooden board at the front of a shot put circle against which an athlete can brace his or her foot.

Diet and nutrition

What you eat and drink daily and in the hours before training or a track and field event can affect you and your performance. Try to eat a major meal at least two-and-a-half to three hours before a competition to give your body a chance to digest your food and get energy from it. Lighter, easily digested foods such as fruit, rice cakes, oatmeal cookies, and plain granola bars can form a small snack during a long track and field meet. All the effort made in training and competition can leave you short of fluids in your body. You should top up regularly with small amounts of water and occasionally fruit juice, but avoid carbonated drinks.

As an athlete, you should be eating a healthy, balanced diet every day. Keep your intake of fast foods with high levels of fat and sugar down to a minimum. Concentrate on eating foods full of protein and complex carbohydrates, such as rice, pasta, noodles, fresh fruit and vegetables, tuna, chicken, and lean meats.

Books

Fundamentals of Track and Field, Gerald A Carr
(Human Kinetics Publishers, 1999)

Olympic Track and Field, Brian Belval
(Rosen Publishing Group, 2007)

Web Sites

Due to the changing nature of Internet links, PowerKids Press has developed an online list of Web Sites related to the subject of this book. This site is updated regularly. Please use this link to access this list:
www.powerkidslinks.com/best/track

INDEX